THE

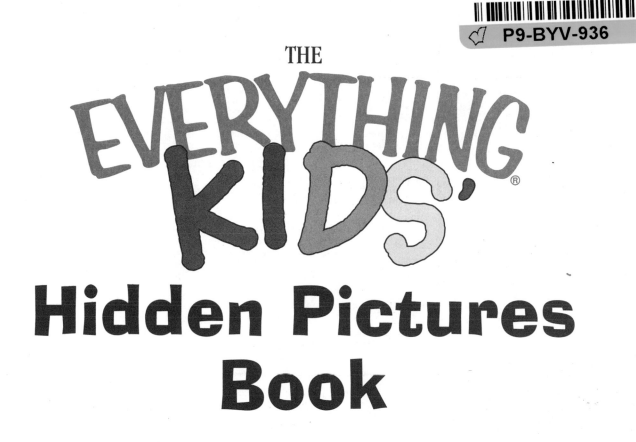

EVERYTHING KIDS'®

Hidden Pictures Book

Hours of challenging fun!

Beth L. Blair

Adams Media

Avon, Massachusetts

EDITORIAL
Publishing Director: Gary M. Krebs
Managing Editor: Kate McBride
Copy Chief: Laura MacLaughlin
Acquisitions Editor: Bethany Brown
Production Editor: Jamie Wielgus

PRODUCTION
Production Director: Susan Beale
Production Manager: Michelle Roy Kelly
Series Designer: Colleen Cunningham
Layout and Graphics: Colleen Cunningham,
    Rachael Eiben, John Paulhus,
    Daria Perreault, Erin Ring
Cover Layout: Paul Beatrice, Frank Rivera

An Everything® Series Book.
Everything® is a registered trademark of F + W Publications, Inc.

Published by Adams Media, an F + W Publications Company
57 Littlefield Street, Avon, MA 02322. U.S.A.
www.adamsmedia.com

ISBN: 1-59337-128-4

Printed in the United States of America.

J   I   H   G   F   E   D   C   B   A

This publication is designed to provide accurate and authoritative information with regard to the subject matter covered. It is sold with the understanding that the publisher is not engaged in rendering legal, accounting, or other professional advice. If legal advice or other expert assistance is required, the services of a competent professional person should be sought.
— From a *Declaration of Principles* jointly adopted
by a Committee of the American Bar Association and a Committee of Publishers and Associations

Many of the designations used by manufacturers and sellers to distinguish their products are claimed as trademarks. Where those designations appear in this book and Adams Media was aware of a trademark claim, the designations have been printed with initial capital letters.

Cover illustrations by Dana Regan.
Interior illustrations by Kurt Dolber.
Puzzles by Beth L. Blair.

This book is available at quantity discounts for bulk purchases.
For information, call 1-800-872-5627.

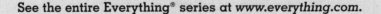

See the entire Everything® series at *www.everything.com*.

Dedication

To my Daddy-o, who taught me to see
the faces hidden everywhere! Love, Beth

Contents

Introduction

When I was a little girl, my favorite holiday was Easter. Not because of the beautiful spring flowers, or the chocolate bunnies, or even the basket of goodies that I amazingly found at the foot of my bed on Easter morning. No, it was the Easter egg hunt that was my all-time favorite part of the holiday! In our house, hiding Easter eggs was an art. We didn't let the Easter bunny do this important task—it belonged to my father alone. He spent a long time finding just the right hiding place for each egg. A pale green egg would disappear into a pale green houseplant. A bright yellow egg would become invisible on top of a bright yellow toy dump truck. The reddest of eggs could barely be seen perched in a bowl of fresh, red tomatoes. One time Dad even taped a bright blue egg onto the perch in the bird cage with our bright blue parakeet! I walked by that egg all morning thinking I was seeing my bird, Joseph, and not the egg I was looking for. My Dad knew the secret of creating the perfect hidden picture puzzle.

I thought of those Easter mornings a lot while I was creating the puzzles in this book. It was a real challenge to figure out how to hide a whale in the branches of a tree, or an elephant in a watering can. It was even harder to turn a person's nose into a trumpet, or a girl's head into a teacup! But if you study any picture long enough, the shapes start to look like all kinds of other things. Suddenly a coat sleeve looks like a wrinkled sock, and a flower looks like a butterfly. With a sharp pencil, and a lot of erasing, it is possible to turn folds and creases, hair and petals, fur and flowers into amazing pictures of totally different things—hidden pictures, that you don't really notice until you look right at them.

I hope you enjoy finding all the crazy things that I've hidden for you in *The Everything® Kids' Hidden Pictures Book*. When you get to the puzzle in the food chapter with the grampa and grandson giggling over the faces they have made with the food on their dinner plates, think of me and my dad. We still do that!

Happy hunting!

Beth L. Blair

For extra fun, see how many hidden pictures you can uncover on the first page of every chapter. There are 23 pictures in all.

Chapter 1
Family Fun

Who's in the family?

Carefully study this picture. Use the hidden clues to figure out how many family members use this kitchen. Pets count, too!

Sorting Laundry

The Murphy boys are doing chores today. Help them answer the following questions:

- Do all the socks match into pairs?
- Which pair of socks is different from all the others?
- Are there more shorts or T-shirts?
- Are the shirts correctly numbered from 1 to 8?

COPY COUSINS

These two cousins look so much alike that people often mistake them for twin sisters. Can you find the 11 differences between the pictures of these cousins and their cats?

HINT: It doesn't count that they are facing in different directions.

family Portrait

Can you find the 12 differences between the two pictures of this family?

Family Reunion

Find the word "HUGS" 11 times in this happy family reunion. See if you can also find the snake, snowman, kite, teapot, snail, umbrella, lightning bolt, and head of a bunny.

Sunday Dinner

Can you find 24
unusual additions to
this funny family feast?

Tea Time

The Thompson kids are having a tea party. Can you find at least 20 things that start with the letter "T"? EXTRA FUN: Try and find 10 more "T" words!

Yard Work

Help the kids find these objects as they rake leaves:
ICECREAM CONE, KITE, RACE CAR, MITTEN,
FISH HEAD, FLAGPOLE, PLAYING CARD,
CAPITAL H, UMBRELLA, TENNIS RACKET,
TEEPEE, STAR, MOUSE, TIC TAC TOE BOARD.

Good Night!

Uncle Chris read Andrew a scary story just before bedtime. Now Andrew sees monsters everywhere! Can you find the seven monsters, and the three words "MONSTER" in his room?

Dish Duty

Kiki and Matt are cleaning up after dinner.

Can you help them find 7 teacups, 3 glasses, 3 forks, and 1 knife?

Silly Shopping

J.T. and his Pops have gone food shopping. Can you see the 19 silly things in this market?

Chapter 2

Perfect Pets

cozy cats

When Mia and Spook sleep in a furry bundle, it's hard to tell where Mia ends and Spook begins! It's also hard to find the following 19 items: leaf, wrist watch, ice cream cone, fish, drum, two drumsticks, ladder, teacup, bunny slipper, hanger, heart, open book, capital H, sailboat, trumpet, sock, butterfly, elf.

Something Fishy

These pets are acting shy. Can you find the 11 fish that are hiding in this tank?

HINT: Don't count the one fish that is colored in for you!!

Pretty Polly

Can you find the five differences between these perky pets?

EXTRA FUN: See if you can also find the hidden football, Christmas stocking, diamond ring, banana, and orange slice.

Look Alikes

Have you noticed that many pet owners look like their pets? Match the pets in the top picture to their people in the bottom picture.

Extra Fun: There are patterns that are the same in both pictures. How many can you see?

EXTRA Extra Fun: Can you find the hidden telephone receiver, teacup, capital M, glove, apple, gingerbread man, and trumpet?

Tons o' Treats

Old Mrs. Hubbard went to the pet store to get her poor dog some bones.
Answer these questions about the goodies that Mrs. Hubbard bought.

1. Are there more dark bones, or light bones?

2. Is there the same number of hot dogs and circle treats?

3. Can you find the one treat that is different than all the rest?

4. If Mrs. Hubbard paid $2.30 for the whole bag of treats, how much does each treat cost?

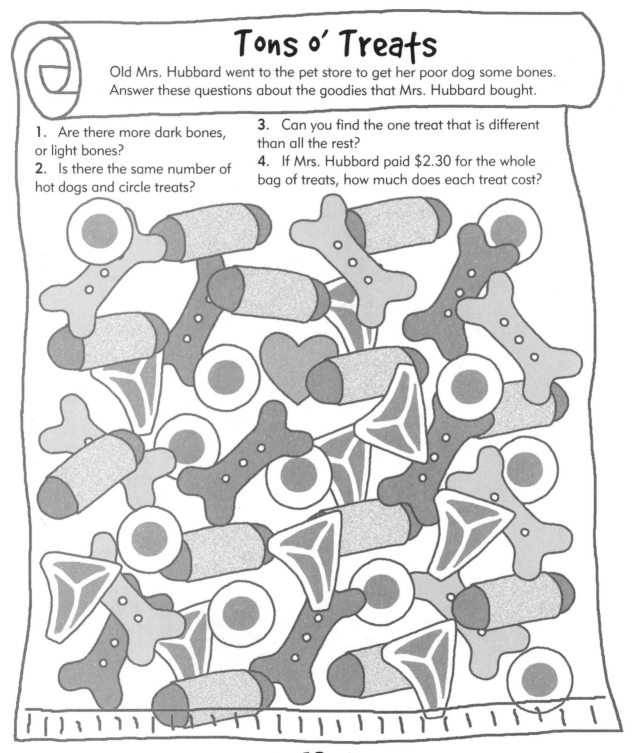

Heidi's Hamster

How many things can you find that begin with the letter H?
EXTRA FUN: Can you find the hidden ice cream cone?

Not Again!

Can you find the 15 escaped snakes?

Scared-y Pets

A lot of pets are scared to go to the vet's.
Can you find the 11 pets hiding in this waiting
room? There are three dogs, three cats, a
snake, a bunny, a lizard, a bird, and a turtle.
HINT: Sometimes you can only see the pet's
face, not the whole body.

How many unusual things can you find in this pet store? While you are looking, see if you can also find the sailboat, Christmas stocking, teacup, ice cream cone, football, comb, flagpole with flag, capital H, capital V, and a banana.

Extra Fun: Which is the biggest pet in the store?

The Pet Store

Happy Hedgehog

Princess Rosabel is a pet hedgehog, and flies are her favorite food. Can you find the nine times the word FLY is written in this picture?

EXTRA FUN: See if you can also find two tulips, two worms, a daisy, a spider, a Christmas tree, a capital W, a capital H, a snail, a banana, a coat hanger, and a spider web.

Dogs in the Yard

Katlyn and the dogs are hanging out, but you have work to do! Find the Christmas tree, comb, maple leaf, head of a fox, piece of pizza, flying saucer, goose, teapot, horse, teacup, bell, scissors, clothespin, pencil, heart, music note, head of a bird, sailboat, ruler, wide-brimmed hat, and Christmas stocking.

Time for a Snack

These friends are enjoying a snack after practice. They are eating cookies, but can you find the 14 other snacks hiding in the picture? Look for a chicken leg, bowl of spaghetti, slice of pizza, can of soda, carrot, orange slice, muffin, ice cream cone, pear, apple, bunch of grapes, hot dog in a bun, sandwich, and a banana.

EEK!

Martin's sister doesn't have a clue that Martin and his friend are hiding behind the sofa. Can you find the other 18 items that are also hiding in this picture?

Look for a pair of eyeglasses, bowling pin, heart, Christmas stocking, flag, comb, golf club, safety pin, umbrella, number 8, glove, gingerbread man, two fish, musical note, snake, banana, and ladder.

OUR CLUB

21

our club

The two friends on the page to the left are hiding up in their tree house. Can you find the following 16 items that are hiding in the picture with them? Look for a butterfly, carrot, paintbrush, snail, belt, horn, baseball cap, pair of scissors, squirrel, paper clip, capital letter E, fork, elephant face, slice of pizza, clothes hanger, and a heart.

Sleepover

These two friends are fast asleep. Can you find everything that one of the girls brought for her sleepover? Look for a backpack, toothbrush, tube of toothpaste, nightgown, book, pair of socks, and a hairbrush.

What's Up?

These two friends are trying to hide the fact that they are passing notes in class. Can you find the other 13 things that are hiding in this classroom? Look for a saucepan, nail, heart, Christmas stocking, sailboat, number 7, number 3, octopus, caterpillar, crown, comb, baseball cap, capital letter J.

crazy Hats

These two friends bought the same crazy hats...or did they? See if you can find five hidden items. Some are in one hat, and some are in the other! You are looking for a referee's whistle, paper clip, heart, wristwatch, banana, and a fried egg.

EXTRA FUN: Now try to find five more differences between the two hats!

funny faces

These friends are having a funny face contest. Who do you think wins? While you are deciding, you can also look for the 15 items hiding in this picture. They are a question mark, party hat, ice cream cone, glove, capital letter E, ball gown, bell, banana, saw, teacup, Christmas tree, capital letter W, flag and flagpole, corn on the cob, and a ski boot.

Where Is the cake?

These friends want some birthday cake. Can you find all 11 slices?

On the Boardwalk

Two friends are enjoying a frozen treat. Can you find at least 15 other things that start with the letters FR?

EXTRA FUN: Find the hidden ice cream bar, pencil, cup, umbrella, and number 3.

FRANK'S FRESH FOOD

"the best on the beach!"

FREE CONCERT

TODAY'S TEMP. 94½°

NEWS @ FRIDAY 10th

TRASH

Pen Pals

Pen pals are friends who may live far away. Can you find at least four clues that tell where this pen pal lives? While you are looking, see if you can also find an umbrella, heart, snake, teacup, numbers 7 and 8, musical note, soup ladle, drinking glass with straw, mitten, carrot, head of a bunny, and a Christmas tree.

Answer these questions about Margaret and Angela's shell collection:

- If all the starfish have five arms, how many arms are there all together?
- Are there more sand dollars or snail shells?
- How many big, spotted shells are there? Are they all the same?

Shell collection

Chapter 4

School Time

Class Picture

Everybody wants to find themselves in the class picture! Can you also find the 28 hidden items? Look for a fan, capital letter H, comb, duck, kite, mitten, lightbulb, flashlight, kneesock, scissors, pickle, cone, glass with straw, smiling face, smiling face with glasses, banana, ladle, safety pin, wristwatch, umbrella, screw, fish, needle and thread, snail, flag on a pole, jellybean, pipe, and a strip of bacon.

Science class

These girls are looking at leaves, but are not seeing the 13 other items hiding in the picture with them. Look for the acorn, Christmas tree, telephone receiver, banana, polar bear, number 6, head of a dog, flamingo, milk pitcher, fork, ruler, heart, and jack o' lantern.

EXTRA FUN: One of the girls is doing more work than the other. Can you figure out who it is?

Math Magic

Can you find the numbers from 0 to 9?

Gross!

The kids in the lunchroom can't hide from this kid's bad manners. But 13 familiar objects can! Look for a canoe, football, saw, teacup, flying bird, spoon, needle and thread, car, gingerbread man, ghost, Christmas stocking, comb, and the head of a crocodile.

Ride the Bus

Look carefully at these two buses and see if you can find the hidden pencil, snail, capital letter E, lightning bolt, umbrella, and book.

EXTRA FUN: See if you can find four other things that are different between the bus on the top and the bus on the bottom.

Book Report

As you read these Tales of Adventure, look for 17 hidden objects. They are a pair of scissors, pair of dice, safety pin, purse, candle, fork, number 3, chicken leg, whale, umbrella, snake, leaf, cup, carrot, jellybean, needle and thread, and a fish hook.

These students see only flowers, but there are 18 other items hiding in this classroom, too. Look for a spool of thread, telephone receiver, mitten, banana, paper clip, capital letters A and E, needle and thread, crown, bow, smiley face, snail, gingerbread man, pencil, sock, book, kite, and a golf club.

Art class

No Homework?

Brian says he can't find a pencil, so he can't do his homework!
There are 13 pencils in this picture. Can you find them?

Homeschool

These homeschool students have filled their kitchen with many projects. There are 12 objects hiding, too. Find the swim flipper, crown, fish, wishbone, pencil, flag on a pole, duck, capital letter H, candy cane, whistle, flashlight, and umbrella.

FIGURE IT OUT: What part of the world are the kids studying?

MATH COUPONS

ATLANTIC OCEAN

PICK UP MORE CLAY

R F I A C A

BROWN

LIFE WITH Lions

Lunch Money

Answer the following questions about the contents of Annie's backpack.

- How much money does **2.00** Annie have to buy lunch?
- Are there more paperclips **yes** than pennies?
- Of which coin is there only one? **Nikes**
- Did Annie remember to bring her house key?

EXTRA FUN:
Look for the gym sock, umbrella, banana, and heart that are also in the backpack.

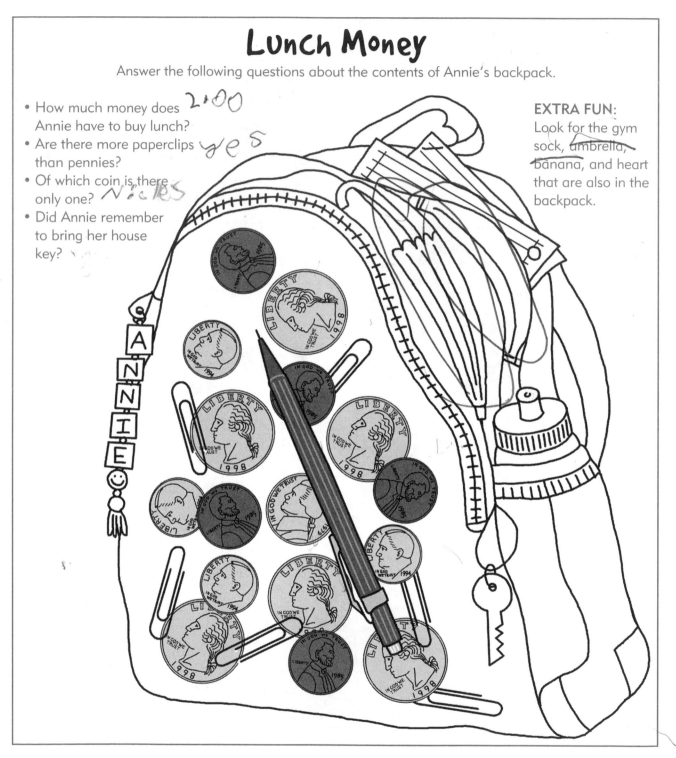

Chapter 5

In the Neighborhood

To Each His Own

In this neighborhood, all the houses are very different from each other. Yet they all have something in common—at least two things hiding in each house or yard! Look for a candle, toothbrush, pair of eyeglasses, Christmas tree, pencil, capital letter E, pair of pants, snake, diamond ring, number 8, gingerbread man, slice of watermelon, needle and thread, giraffe, playing card, duck, soda can with straw, mitten, the word HOUSE, and a wristwatch.

Look Alikes

Colin is going to visit a friend in a brand new neighborhood. But all the houses look so much alike, how will Colin's dad know where to drop him off? "Don't worry," says the friend. "We're the only house that has lots of flowers, and a white dog. Plus, we marked our house with an 'A' so all our friends will be able to find us!" Can you find the correct house?

EXTRA FUN: Colin's friend has lost his kite somewhere. Can you find that, too?

Community Cool

These kids are having a great time in the neighborhood pool. But 15 items are swimming with them that don't belong there! Find the candle, snake, capital letter L, teacup, sock, planet Saturn, jug, referee's whistle, bat, musical note, pickle, sneaker, kite, number 6, and the word SWIM.

Hello, Neighbor!

Min Joo can see her neighbors walking by, but there are 17 other items in this picture that she can't see! Find the comb, scissors, flying saucer, telephone receiver, teacup, mitten, heart, balloon, golf tee, ruler, hammer, guitar, sock, toothbrush, fishhook, smiley face, and cane.

Welcome Home!

Keep the Neighborhood Clean

Answer these questions about what the neighbors found
on their annual Clean-Up Day in the park. Did they find . . .

. . . more choco milk cartons or cola cans?
. . . which was the most popular drink?
. . . as many bottle caps as bottles?
. . . as many straws as drink containers?
. . . which was the least popular treat?

Welcome Home!

Juan's neighbors have just brought home their new baby. Juan and his family have prepared a few presents to surprise them. However, the big surprise is that there are 16 unexpected presents for the baby hiding in the picture to the left! Look for a toy bird, a rattle, two baby booties, a bottle, a baby carriage, two mittens, a pacifier, three diaper pins, a baby hat with pompom, a blanket with satin edge, a disposable diaper, and a rubber ducky.

In the Park

These kids are enjoying the park in their city neighborhood. Can you find the 13 items that are hiding in the park with them? Look for a caterpillar, capital letters A and E, teapot, book, ghost, heart, sock, question mark, ladder, banana, kite, and a glove.

City Scenes

This city neighborhood has lots to do. But there are 13 creatures who have moved into town from their country neighborhoods. Can you find them hiding between all the activity? Look for a chicken, goldfish, mouse, snake, butterfly, giraffe, frog, turtle, bunny, swan, whale, bat, and a hedgehog.

oops!

Daryl's neighborhood lemonade sale was going pretty good until Stormy the dog came to visit! Now most of his lemonade is gone. Daryl is also missing three lemon slices, and the word LEMON 14 times. Can you help Daryl with his search?

Andrew wants to unpack his stuff, but everything got jumbled in the move to his new neighborhood! Help Andrew find his sailboat, trumpet, in-line skates, clock, tennis racket, baseball bat, dice, pirate hat, kite, book, hockey stick, piano keyboard, baseball glove, framed photo, flippers, two crayons, computer monitor, bowling pin, four playing cards, pickup truck, candy cane, three jacks, referee whistle, megaphone, ghost costume, and tennis ball.

New in Town

Book Hunt

Jenny and Beth have been going to the neighborhood library since they were six years old!

Today they seem to have misplaced the books they took out. Can you find all 15 books in this picture?

HINT: Some books are very small, and some are very large!

Chapter 6

On Vacation

School's out!

These kids can't hide how happy they are to be out of school for a whole week! What they can't see is that hiding in the picture with them are 12 ideas for having fun when you have some time away from school work. Look for a kite, ski boot, hockey stick, slice of pizza, movie ticket, paper airplane, jump rope, skateboard, football, music note, fishing pole, and (last on the list) a T.V.!

catch Some ZZZs

Vacation is a great time for hiding out under the covers. Can you find the other items that are hiding in this picture, too? Look for a sock, pair of dice, needle and thread, kite, sweatshirt, soda can and straw, heart, baby elephant's face, clock, spider, spider web, fish, and 13 Zs!

Dad's Famous Pancakes

During vacation, there's a lot more time for breakfast! While you're watching this pancake loop-the-loop, look out for 12 other early morning items: a comb, strip of bacon, peach, toothbrush, tube of toothpaste, fried egg, two coffee mugs, banana, knife with pat of butter, fork, and a heart (because dad just LOVES to flip pancakes)!

PICK UP MILK

EGGS

BUTTER

1 3 5

Armchair Adventures

When you're on vacation, its OK to stay up late and finish a really good book! This boy is reading a collection of 16 different adventure stories. See if you can find the following items from his book hiding in this picture: whale, Native American peace pipe, planet Saturn, rocket ship, mermaid, sailboat, fishing pole, knight in armor, hang glider, hot air balloon, pyramid, castle, ghost, snake, mountains, elephant.

Pack Your Bags!

These girls are getting ready for their vacation. Can you find at least eight shapes that are the same in both pictures? Be careful, the shape may be the same, but it might be used in a totally different way!

EXTRA FUN:
Take another look. What do you notice that is the opposite between these pictures?

Road Trip

Dad is still trying to stuff the last few items into the back of the family van. Can you find 11 more hidden items that this family is taking along on their vacation? Look for a paperclip, needle and thread, slice of bread, pear, hammer, pencil, adhesive bandage, light bulb, clock, phone receiver, and a coffee mug.

creature feature

These kids have all rushed to see the new scary movie released on the first day of vacation. They are so interested in the monsters on the screen, that they don't notice any of the 16 creepy items sitting right in the theater with them! Look for three ghosts, three bats, two jack o' lanterns, two crawling hands, one set of vampire fangs, and one each of monster eye, cyclops, tombstone, skull, and a bone.

Lazy Days

Summer vacation days are perfect for just hanging out. Can you find the 14 crazy items these boys are imagining they see in the clouds and water? Look for a fancy goldfish, sock, sea monster, dog's face, giraffe, car, two-masted sailboat, whale, guitar, heart, ice cream cone, flying bird, old man's face, and a duck.

Check It Out!

This family is having a great vacation somewhere in the United States. By looking at the clues in the picture, can you figure out what state they are visiting?

EXTRA FUN: A famous scientist who worked with plants was born in this state. His name was George Washington Carver, and he figured out 325 different uses for the peanut! See if you can find the 18 peanuts hiding in this picture.

Wish You Were Here

Your friend is on vacation in North Carolina and sent you two of the same postcards. But are they really the same? See if you can find the following hidden items:

fish hook
mitten
needle
kite
letter E

EXTRA FUN:
After you find all of the hidden items, see if you can find five other ways in which these cards are different!

California Dreamin'

Sometimes it is really hard to *stop* being on vacation!
One boy at the bus stop is NOT thinking about snow,
math, history, or going back to school. Can you find the
hidden word that describes what is on his mind?
HINT: Unscramble the letters below to help you in your search.

N H U S S N I E

Chapter 7

Let's Eat

What Smells So Good?

It is really hard to hide from the heavenly aroma of a backyard barbecue! However, there are 17 items doing a good job of hiding in this backyard. Can you find them? Look for a rubber duck, mitten, kite, candle, sleepy man in the moon, chess piece, pencil, closed umbrella, ski, golf club, horseshoe, bowling pin, wishbone, needle and thread, paper clip, profile of a man's face, and a jug.

Summer sweet corn is so good that it's hard to imagine eating anything else! In fact, these folks are so busy eating corn that they don't seem to notice the 15 other tasty foods hiding in the picture with them. See if you can find the bagel, orange, ice cream cone, ice cream bar, candy cane, chicken leg, slice of pizza, banana, slice of bread, jellybean, fried egg, a pod full of peas, carrot, strawberry, and a dog bone (for the family friend)!

Can't Get Enough Sweet Corn

Silly Chefs

Can you find nine words that might be used when describing the creations these silly chefs are cooking up? Look for: yum, slurp, delicious, good, tasty, munch, wonderful, sweet, and hot.

Extra Fun: While you are browsing in this kitchen, also look for the hidden knife, fork, oven mitt, cookbook, and measuring cup.

Scoops

Can you find the 19 items that you might not want to mix with ice cream? Look for a snail, bird, mitten, umbrella, paperclip, cat's face, ghost, number 3, gingerbread man, fried egg, comb, pencil, earthworm, slice of bacon, horn, bubble pipe, snowman's face, pickle, and a rocket ship.

Sneaking Treats

The kids all love Gramma Ginny's cookies. They're trying to sneak a few while they're still hot from the oven! Can you find the 17 other items that have snuck into this picture, too? Look for a book, gingerbread man, banana, teacup, sock, ladder, glove, three pieces of popcorn, coat hanger, candy cane, traffic light, umbrella, referee's whistle, domino, and a turtle?

Just One Bite—Please?

This big brother is being pretty patient, but the baby just doesn't want to eat lunch! Maybe he should take a break and see if he can find the 15 items hiding in the kitchen instead. There's a musical note, ghost, comb, safety pin, car, flag, tube of toothpaste, capital letter L and capital letter M, paintbrush, thimble, fork, butterfly, cherry, and a rubber duck.

Grams is not happy to see that the "boys" are making faces with their food! She would be even less pleased to see the other 12 faces hiding in this picture! Can you find them? Look for a bear, crocodile, frog, cat, owl, mouse, elephant, witch, puppy, man in the moon, bald man, and a man with a long nose.

Food Fun

Jesse is showing his friends how to make his favorite "bunny salad." In fact, bunnies like this salad so much, that bunches of them are hiding in the picture waiting for a taste! Can you find all 20 bunny faces?

EXTRA FUN: A bunny salad is simple to make. A canned pear half is the bunny body, cottage cheese is the tail, half a cherry is the nose, two long slices of banana are the ears, and the eyes are raisins.

Bunny Salad

Super Salad

You might find all sorts of goodies hiding in a big bowl of salad—but you probably wouldn't want to see the following 21 items! Search among the lettuce leaves and see if you can find a thimble, needle and thread, bug, bunny face, crown, bicycle, diamond, baseball cap, goldfish, spring, pair of eyeglasses, hatchet, bat, kite, two jacks, glove, clown's face, balloon, star, and a Christmas tree!

Hiding Hot Dogs

The family pets have found the perfect place to hide. Under the table it's quiet, dark, and people drop all kinds of good food down to you! See if you can find the other 11 items hiding in this picture. Look for a bubble pipe, musical note, hot dog in a bun, goose, golf club, cane, diamond, domino, bat, bowling pin, and a heart.

Saying Grace

This family is pausing to give thanks for the food they are about to eat. Look carefully at the picture. Can you find the five hidden words that complete the simple grace to the right? Write the words on the lines provided.

God is _____.

God is _____.

Let us _____ *Him*

For our _____.

_____

Chapter 8

The Great Outdoors

The Bike Path

The tall flags on the back of these kids' bikes help other bikers and walkers see them coming. What they can't see, however, are the 20 other items hiding in this picture! Look for a carrot, rubber duck, pair of scissors, rowboat, snake, kite, piece of pie, pair of eyeglasses, balloon, spoon, coat hanger, snail, jellyfish, capital letter G, ice cream cone, bird, crown, ladder, whistle, and a teacup.

Berry Picking?

Can you find the 20 items hiding in the berry patch? Look for a bee, butterfly, piece of pie, shovel, spider, light bulb, gingerbread man, bat, spoon, teacup, hanger, bubble pipe, harp, flag, car, paintbrush, ice cream cone, frog, golf club, and a banana.

Bird Watching

Sometimes if you're very quiet, you can see where a mother bird has hidden her nest. Try to find the following items that are hiding in the trees with her! Look for a bunny, sock, heart, whale, kite, crown, pair of dice, three jacks, mitten, teapot, star, and a pair of scissors.

Creepy Crawlies

These kids found a lot of interesting things to study outside. Can you find the 15 items hiding in the picture, too? Look for a whistle, umbrella, heart, bowling pin, snake, wishbone, toothbrush, banana, sword, pickle, spider, teacup, spoon, horn, and a slice of bacon.

Downhill Race

These kids want to see who can make it down the hill first. They don't know that there are 17 hidden items racing down the hill with them! See if you can find the snake, star, beaver, question mark, angel, sock, kite, umbrella, pair of dice, fish hook, comb, capital letter W, caterpillar, light bulb, camera, and an ice cream cone.

Summer Nights

The fireflies that these kids are trying to catch are easy
to see because they are flashing brightly. It is not so
easy to see the 17 items that are hidden in this dark
yard. See if you can find a broom, glove, gingerbread
man, heart, umbrella, clothespin, wooden bucket, cane,
ruler, pair of scissors, bow, toadstool, book, spoon,
horseshoe, man's profile, and "The Big Dipper"!

City Garden

This girl may have a tiny garden, but there are lots of hiding places there! Look for a parrot, a pair of glasses, a fish, another fish, comb, kite, bow, candle, hammer, capital letter E, butterfly, sock, capital letter L, lunchbox, baby elephant's face, and a bunny's face.

Soccer Scramble

Sometimes there are so many kids out running around the field that everyone gets all mixed up! Can you find the six separate soccer players in this crazy game? Look carefully—the players may overlap each other.

Rain Dance

What a lovely, splashy day to go out and play! See if you can find the following (very wet) items hidden in this picture: the word RAIN seven times, a rubber duck, jellyfish, boot, rainbow, eye, smiley face, witch face, golf club, needle and thread, heart, frog, and a bell.

The Swimmin' Hole

These kids like to hide out at their favorite pond on a hot summer's day. Can you see the 20 items that are hiding here, too? Look for a turtle, snake, snail, fish, needle and thread, kite, saucepan, teacup, witch's face, referee's whistle, frog's face, flag, two rocket ships, a star, spoon, bowling pin, spider, crown, and a paintbrush.

Scavenger Hunt

Answer these questions about the items Kate found in her backyard:

- Did Kate find more smooth white stones, or smooth dark stones?
- How many acorns did she find? Do all the acorns have their caps?
- Kate found only one of something. What is it?
- Add together the number of feathers, twigs, and pinecones. Can you divide the answer by the number 2?

Chapter 9

Indoor Adventures

Can you find the seven kids and three cats hiding in this room? While you are searching, see if you can also find a kite, book of matches, golf club, hot dog in a bun, book, postage stamp, pencil, capital letter M, spoon, paper clip, and a candle.

Hide and Seek

Pinball Wizard

How many points will this boy win at pinball? Add up all the numbers you can find hiding in the picture to find out! **EXTRA FUN:** Find an umbrella, party hat, domino, banana, snail shell, and slice of bread.

Look Alikes

See if you can find shapes and patterns that are the same in both pictures. **HINT**: The shape might be the same, but the way it is used might be completely different! For example, the cloud in the top picture is the same shape as the icing on the cupcake in the bottom picture!

Practice, Practice, Practice

You may need to practice your detective skills to find the 13 musical notes hidden in this picture! **EXTRA FUN:** While you are looking for the notes, see if you can also find the hang glider, traffic light, needle, bowling pin, owl, rubber duck, and Christmas tree.

Clean Your Room!

This girl is taking a break to read an old comic book she found while cleaning her room. See if you can find the following 16 items that are still hiding in the junk! Look for a clothespin, question mark, capital letter Y, acorn, banana, domino, fish hook, paintbrush, teacup, flag, rubber duck, pointy winter hat, camera, ice cream cone, car, and a fish.

Tent City

When it's a really rainy day outside, what's a good way to have fun? Hide inside your own tent city! See if you can find 15 items hiding with the kids. Look for a Christmas stocking, banana, flag, spider web, mitten, snake, needle and thread, ghost, domino, thimble, ladder, picture frame, old fashioned soda bottle, paper clip, and a sailboat.

Whose Turn Is It?

Oh dear! The cat has totally messed up the kids' game. Not only that, all the game pieces are lost. Can you find the five heart-shaped and five star-shaped game pieces hiding in this mess? See if you can locate the pair of dice, too.

Huh?

If you spend a day inside an art gallery, you will see some very interesting things! Search this painting to find a teacup, snail, car, umbrella, candy cane, rubber duck, Christmas stocking, winter cap, music note, Christmas tree, diamond, the number 2, paper clip, G clef, and (of course) the cow!

Title: The Cow

In the Attic

These kids found some great clothes hiding in the attic. Can you find the 14 items hiding in the clothes?

Look for:

bunny face

guitar

wishbone

scissors

sock

kite

bat

ladder

carrot

flag

glass

spider

spider web

pencil

Word Search

To figure out what activities these kids are enjoying, unscramble the words below. Then find the words hidden in the picture.

1. NRBAI EETASSR
2. NEIHDD SRCPITUE
3. DRGIS
4. SMGAE

5. EOJKS
6. ZEZPULS
7. EDIRDLS
8. ZAEMS

EXTRA FUN:
Can you figure out how to write the puzzle name "dot to dot" without using any letters? When you have, look for the answer hiding in the picture!

crafty cat

This cat is trying, but he's not quite as well hidden as the 13 other items in this picture! Look for a heart, candy cane, slice of bread, bat, fish hook, pickle, chicken, earthworm, diamond, house key, kite, ice cream cone, and a Christmas tree.

APPENDIX A

Now Where Did I See That . . . ?

There are almost 100 different picture puzzles in this book. Each one has at least ten items hiding in it. That's a *lot* of hidden pictures—but you're not done looking yet! See if you can find each of these nine picture pieces somewhere in this book. Write the name of the puzzle each piece is from in the space under each box. **HINT:** There is only one picture piece from each chapter.

1.

2.

3.

4.

5.

6.

7.

8.

9.

APPENDIX B

Online Resources

✎ *www.kids-puzzles.com*

The hidden picture puzzles at this site look like ordinary black-and-white drawings. But when you find one of the hidden objects and click on it, the object pops into full color and moves across the page to take its place in the list of objects you are looking for! A hidden sock will walk across the page, a hidden snake will slither across the page, a hidden ball will bounce across the page, etc. This site also has a section of hidden picture problems (a picture appears as you complete the math equations), connect-the-dot puzzles, matching games, word search puzzles, and mazes! Note: Your computer will need the FLASH 6 plug-in for you to view this site. Ask an adult to help with the easy download.

✎ *www.niehs.nih.gov/kids/home.htm*

This fun site was prepared by the National Institute of Environmental Health Sciences. Once you get to the home page, click on the link for Hidden Pictures. After you have found all the objects in each picture, you can color the picture online, too! Explore additional links for Sing-a-Long songs, Brainteasers and Riddles, Storytime, and Humor and Jokes. Puzzles also available in Spanish. Note: Your computer will need a Java-enabled browser like Netscape or Microsoft Explorer for you to play many of these games.

✎ *www.wimzie.com*

Once you get to the home page, follow the links from "Kids", to "Wimzie Activities", to "Horace's Hidden Pictures." Based on characters from the popular kids TV puppet show "Wimzie's House", these puzzles might look like they are for younger kids, but they are fun for all! As you click on each hidden object, it pops into full color, and the list counts down to let you know how many objects you have left to find. You can also print out the puzzles and do them on paper with a pencil if you would rather.

✎ *www.las-cruces.org/airport/kids5.html*

Sponsored by the Las Cruces International Airport in New Mexico. The site has six really fun hidden picture puzzles that each feature flying. Look at the puzzles online, or print them out for free.

✎ *www.highlightskids.com*

This is a great site, but it does cost about $30 a year to subscribe. If they agree to the fee, a parent or an adult would have to sign you up. Subscribers receive a new selection of online, interactive, hidden picture puzzles each month, as well as mystery messages, picture-twister games, and an on-line "maze maker." However, if you want to try one of *Highlights* super fun hidden picture puzzles for FREE, just go to the site listed above, and click on the link for "sample."

Printed Resources

Animal Hidden Pictures, by Cheryl Nathan. Dover Coloring Book, Dover Publications, Mineola, NY, 2002.

This book has 14 different hidden picture puzzles. Each puzzle features a different kind of animal, such as giraffes, lions, ostriches, rhinos, crocodiles, and more!

Ultimate Hidden Pictures, by Tony and Tony Tallarico. Price Stern Sloan, a division of Penguin Putnam Books for Young Readers, New York, NY, 2003.

Most of these big puzzles cover two full pages. Each puzzle is chock full of crazy characters having silly conversations, as well as tons of hidden objects. Topics include "Across America", "Halloween", "Under the Sea", sports, dinosaurs, and Christmas.

Highlights Hidden Pictures 2003–2004, Volume 1, Boyds Mills Press, PA.

This is a great selection of hidden picture puzzles done by a variety of different artists. Each puzzle includes a list with pictures of the objects you are looking for.

Super Colossal Book of Hidden Pictures, Volume 2, Boyds Mills Press, PA, 2001.

Compiled by the editors of *Highlights* magazine, this book has more than 150 pages of puzzles, with more than 2,000 objects to find!

The Mighty Big Book of Optical Illusions, by Craig Yoe. Price Stern Sloan, a division of Penguin Putnam Books for Young Readers, New York, NY, 2002.

You might not think of optical illusions in the same category as hidden picture puzzles, but many of them are! Do you see a magician or a rabbit? An old lady or a pretty young girl? Is this man playing a banjo, or a flute? It's all in the way you look at it!

PUZZLE ANSWERS

page 2 • **Who's in the Family?**

There are five people and three pets in this family: Dad, Mom, Grandmother, school-age child, baby, dog, cat, goldfish. Hints: Look at the pairs of shoes, the coats and hats, the mugs and card on the table, the balloons, the pet dishes and poster on the fridge.

page 3 • **Sorting Laundry**

1. Only one pair of long socks has three stripes at the top.
2. No. Shirt number 4 is missing.
3. There are 12 long socks, which make 6 perfect pairs. There are only 11 short socks, which makes 5 pairs plus 1 extra.
4. There are more shorts (8) than T-shirts (7).

page 4 • **Copy Cousins**

page 5 • **Family Portrait**

PUZZLE ANSWERS

page 6 • Family Reunion

page 7 • Sunday Dinner

page 8 • Tea Time

top hat, three, teeth, thumb, teacup, triangles, tassles, tablecloth, teapot, treats, teaspoon, turtleneck, tiara, turtle, telephone, thumbtack, tree, tulips, tabby cat, tail, table, teddy bear, tie, tile floor, truck, tires, top, tag, tricycle, tennis ball, toy soldier, trumpet, toes, TV.

page 9 • Yard Work

PUZZLE ANSWERS

page 10 • **Good Night!**

page 11 • **Dish Duty**

page 12 • **Silly Shopping**

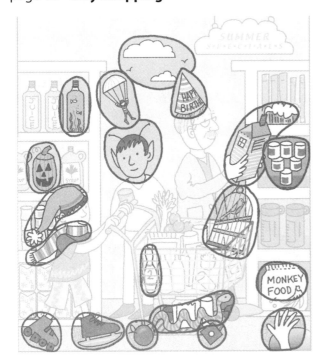

page 14 • **Cozy Cats**

PUZZLE ANSWERS

page 15 • **Something Fishy**

page 16 • **Pretty Polly**

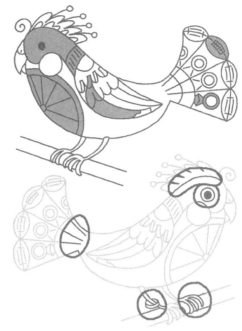

page 17 • **Look Alikes**

page 18 • **Tons o' Treats**

1. There are seven light bones, and only six dark bones.
2. There are 12 hot dogs, and only 11 circles.
3. There is only one heart-shaped treat.
4. There are 46 total treats. $2.30 divided by 46 comes to .05 cents per treat.

page 19 • **Heidi's Hamster**

halo, harp, handlebars, handwriting, hammer, headdress, hamburger, hat, houseplant, hill, hook, handbag, hearing aid, hair, "H" charm, hem, hamper, heart, Harvey the hamster, hand, hoop, horse, half an apple, homework, hairbrush, handle, hole, house, hallway, hood, headlight, hexagon, hen, helium balloon, "happy". Ice cream cone is in the lower left-hand corner, upside-down on the handbag.

PUZZLE ANSWERS

page 20 • **Not Again!**

page 21 • **Scared-y Pets**

page 22 • **The Pet Store**

Unusual things: monkey reading newspaper; toy chicken in cage; fried eggs in cage with chicken; fish bones in fish bowl; cat sleeping in the aquarium; mouse on square exercise wheel, two-headed snake; turtle with a box shell; snail with a clock shell; dog wearing glasses, a beanie, and bunny slippers; cat with an umbrella tail; ferrets wearing hats and scarves; striped flamingo.

EXTRA FUN: The largest animal in the pet store is the elephant, who is hiding on the left side of the page. He's so big, you can only see his trunk and the tip of his tusk!

PUZZLE ANSWERS

page 23 • **Happy Hedgehog**

page 24 • **Dogs in the Yard**

page 26 • **Time for a Snack**

page 27 • **EEK!**

PUZZLE ANSWERS

page 28 • **Our Club**

page 29 • **Sleepover**

page 30 • **What's Up?**

page 31 • **Crazy Hats**

PUZZLE ANSWERS

page 32 • **Funny Faces**

page 33 • **Where Is the Cake?**

page 34 • **On the Boardwalk**

Frank's, Fresh, French fries, FREE concert, French horn, frankfurter, front teeth, frog, fringed skirt, fried egg, fruit, frizzy hair, freckles, frown, frayed jeans, fraction, three fern fronds, frame, Frisbee, Friday's paper.

page 35 • **Pen Pals**

This pen pal lives in Australia! The eight clues are: the Australian flag; poster of a koala bear; toy kangaroo; letter addressed "G'day John,"; book on the history of Ayers Rock; sports shirt for the Canberra team; mask on the wall; pennant for the "Wallabies."

PUZZLE ANSWERS

page 36 • **Shell Collection**

There are seven starfish. If each starfish has five arms, that makes 35 arms all together. There are nine sand dollars and seven snail shells. There are six large, spotted shells, and they are not all the same. The one in the lower left-hand corner of the picture is a very different shape from the others!

page 39 • **Science Class**

The girl looking through the microscope is doing more science work than the girl drawing a clown.

page 38 • **Class Picture**

page 40 • **Math Magic**

PUZZLE ANSWERS

page 41 • **Gross!**

page 42 • **Ride the Bus**

page 43 • **Book Report**

page 44 • **Art Class**

PUZZLE ANSWERS

page 45 • **No Homework?**

page 46 • **Homeschool**

These homeschool students are studying the continent of Africa, and its many different animals; the map on the fridge shows the shape of the continent; giraffes, lions, and elephants all live in Africa; the magnets on the fridge are the letters that spell "Africa."

page 47 • **Spelling Bee**

buzz cut hair, boy scout, bandana, badge, button, belt, back, beaver, blackboard, box of chalk, baseball cap, bowtie, book, bookmark, backpack, bag, banner, bench, braid, barrette, bangs, ballerina, bracelets, ballet shoes, border, basketball, bald, bell bottom pants, beard, bandage, balloon.

page 48 • **Lunch Money**

Annie has $2.00 to buy lunch; there are five pennies and six paperclips; there is only one nickel; yes, today Annie remembered her key!

PUZZLE ANSWERS

page 50 • **To Each His Own**

page 51 • **Look Alikes**

page 52 • **Community Cool**

page 53 • **Hello, Neighbor!**

PUZZLE ANSWERS

page 54 • **Welcome Home!**

page 55 • **Keep the Neighborhood Clean**

1. There were six choco milk cartons and six cola cans.
2. Orange soda was the most popular drink. There were eight bottles.
3. Yes, there were eight bottle caps and eight bottles.
4. No, there were only five straws, but 20 drink containers!
5. Gum was the least popular treat. There were only four gum wrappers.

page 56 • **In the Park**

page 57 • **City Scenes**

page 58 • **Oops!**

PUZZLE ANSWERS

page 59 • **New in Town**

page 60 • **Book Hunt**

page 62 • **School's Out!**

page 63 • **Catch Some ZZZs**

PUZZLE ANSWERS

page 64 • Dad's Famous Pancakes

page 65 • Armchair Adventures

page 66 • Pack Your Bags!

Things that are the SAME: Cage on the ski pole is the same as the beach ball; ski hat is the same as sleeve of Hawaiian shirt; sole of ski boot is the same as sandal; Ski Snow Mountain brochure is same shape as kite; sun on Ski Sun Mtn. brochure same as sum on bathing suit; mitten same as pattern on kite; snowflake on SKI brochure same as snowflake on sweater; pattern on skis same as pattern on palm tree; daisy on T-shirt same as daisy on sun hat.

Things that are OPPOSITE: The girl in the top picture is wearing a T-shirt, but is packing to go on a cold and snowy vacation, while the other girl is wearing a turtleneck sweater, but is packing for a warm and sunny vacation. The first girl is going to learn to ski on snow, while the girl in the lower right is going to learn how to water ski!

page 67 • Road Trip

PUZZLE ANSWERS

page 68 • **Creature Feature**

page 69 • **Lazy Days**

page 70 • **Check It Out!**

page 71 • **Wish You Were Here**

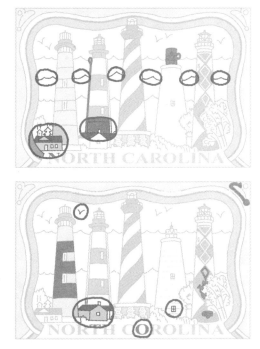

This family is visiting the sate of Missouri. Missouri is known as the "Show Me State" (slogan on the boy's T-shirt). "The Gateway Arch" (Dad's T-shirt) is located in the city of St. Louis, and is the tallest monument in the US. The "world's first ice cream cone" (sign) was said to be sold at the St. Louis World's Fair in 1904. Famous Author "Mark Twain" (girl's T-shirt) author of *Tom Sawyer* and *The Adventures of Huckleberry Finn*, was born in Hannibal, MO. "Paddlewheelers" (gift bag) are a famous type of river boat that once traveled up and down the rivers of Missouri transporting goods, passengers, and entertainment.

PUZZLE ANSWERS

page 72 • California Dreamin'

page 74 • What Smells So Good?

page 75 • Can't Get Enough Sweet Corn

page 76 • Silly Chefs

page 77 • Scoops

PUZZLE ANSWERS

page 78 • **Sneaking Treats**

page 79 • **Just One Bite—Please?**

page 80 • **Food Fun**

page 81 • **Bunny Salad**

PUZZLE ANSWERS

page 82 • **Super Salad**

page 83 • **Hiding Hot Dogs**

page 84 • **Saying Grace**

God is _GREAT_.
God is _GOOD_.
Let us _THANK_ Him
For our _FOOD_.
AMEN

page 86 • **The Bike Path**

PUZZLE ANSWERS

page 87 • **Berry Picking?**

page 88 • **Bird Watching**

page 89 • **Creepy Crawlies**

page 90 • **Downhill Race**

page 91 • **Summer Nights**

★ ★ **131** ★ ★

PUZZLE ANSWERS

page 92 • City Garden

page 93• Soccer Scramble

page 94 • Rain Dance

page 95 • The Swimmin' Hole

page 96 •
Scavenger Hunt

1. Kate found four white stones, but only three dark stones.

2. Kate found six acorns, but only five of them had their caps on.

3. Kate found only one "Polly nose." A Polly nose is the seed pod from the maple tree. If you break one apart in the middle, and peel open the fat end where the seed is, the inside edges of the pod are sticky. You can stick the pod on the end of your nose!

4. No. There are three feathers, three twigs, and five pinecones. That adds up to 11, and you cannot divide 11 by 2 evenly.

PUZZLE ANSWERS

page 98 • Hide and Seek

page 99 • Pinball Wizard

The numbers 1 through 8 are hiding in the picture. If you add them up you get 36 points!

page 100 • Look Alikes

All the circled objects and patterns in the top picture are repeated in the bottom picture.

page 101 • Practice, Practice, Practice

PUZZLE ANSWERS

page 102 • **Clean Your Room!**

page 103 • **Tent City**

page 104 • **Whose Turn Is It?**

page 105 • **Huh?**

PUZZLE ANSWERS

page 106 • In the Attic

page 107 • Word Search

EXTRA FUN: The puzzle name "dot to dot" can be written without using letters by drawing two dots and the number 2, like this, "•2•".

1. BRAIN TEASERS
2. HIDDEN PICTURES
3. GRIDS
4. GAMES
5. JOKES
6. PUZZLES
7. RIDDLES
8. MAZES

page 108 • Crafty Cat

page109 • Now Where Did I See That . . . ?

1. Family Portrait
2. Not Again!
3. Pen Pals
4. Art Class
5. Book Hunt
6. California Dreaming
7. Just One Bite
8. The Swimmin' Hole
9. Look Alikes

THE EVERYTHING® KIDS' SERIES!

Packed with tons of information, activities, and puzzles, the Everything® Kids' books are perennial bestsellers that keep kids active and engaged. Each book is 8" x 9 ¼", 144 pages, and two-color throughout.

All this at the incredible price of $6.95!

The Everything® Kids' Knock Knock Book
1-59337-127-6 ($9.95 CAN)

The Everything® Kids' Hidden Pictures Book
1-59337-128-4 ($9.95 CAN)

The Everything® Kids' Baseball Book, 3rd Ed.
1-59337-070-9

The Everything® Kids' Bible Trivia Book
1-59337-031-8

The Everything® Kids' Bugs Book
1-58062-892-3

The Everything® Kids' Christmas Puzzle &
Activity Book
1-58062-965-2

The Everything® Kids' Cookbook
1-58062-658-0

The Everything® Kids' Halloween Puzzle &
Activity Book
1-58062-959-8

The Everything® Kids' Joke Book
1-58062-686-6

The Everything® Kids' Math Puzzles Book
1-58062-773-0

The Everything® Kids' Mazes Book
1-58062-558-4

The Everything® Kids' Money Book
1-58062-685-8 ($11.95 CAN)

The Everything® Kids' Monsters Book
1-58062-657-2

The Everything® Kids' Nature Book
1-58062-684-X ($11.95 CAN)

The Everything® Kids' Puzzle Book
1-58062-687-4

The Everything® Kids' Riddles & Brain Teasers Book
1-59337-036-9

The Everything® Kids' Science Experiments Book
1-58062-557-6

The Everything® Kids' Soccer Book
1-58062-642-4

The Everything® Kids' Travel Activity Book
1-58062-641-6

All Kids' titles are priced at $6.95 ($10.95 CAN) unless otherwise noted.

The Everything® Bedtime Story Book

by Mark Binder

The Everything® *Bedtime Story Book* is a wonderfully original collection of 100 stories that will delight the entire family. Accompanied by charming illustrations, the stories included are retold in an exceptionally amusing style and are perfect for reading aloud. From familiar nursery rhymes to condensed American classics, this collection promises to promote sweet dreams, active imaginations, and quality family time.

The Everything® Mother Goose Book

by June Rifkin

The Everything® *Mother Goose Book* is a delightful collection of 300 nursery rhymes that will entertain adults and children alike. These wonderful rhymes are easy for even young readers to enjoy—and great for reading aloud. Each page is decorated with captivating drawings of beloved characters. Ideal for any age, *The Everything*® *Mother Goose Book* will inspire young readers and take parents on an enchanting trip down memory lane.

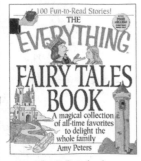

The Everything® Fairy Tales Book

by Amy Peters

Take your children to magical lands where animals talk, mythical creatures wander freely, and good and evil come in every imaginable form. You'll find all this and more in *The Everything*® *Fairy Tales Book*, an extensive collection of 100 classic fairy tales. This enchanting compilation features charming, original illustrations that guarantee creative imaginations and quality family time.